S0-BKG-856

PRESENTED TO

ON THE OCCASION OF

FROM

DATE

A LITTLE INSPIRATION

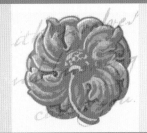

FOR A *Love* FILLED DAY

BARBOUR
PUBLISHING

DEDICATED TO MY husband,
DARRYL, WHO HAS BEEN THE
BLESSING OF TRUE LOVE.

© 2003 by Barbour Publishing, Inc.

ISBN 1-59310-232-1

Compiled by Cynthia Margaret Stoker Franklin.

All Scripture quotations are taken from the King James Version of the Bible.

Published by Barbour Publishing, Inc., P.O. Box 719, Uhrichsville, Ohio 44683, www.barbourbooks.com

*Our mission is to publish and distribute inspirational products offering exceptional value
and biblical encouragement to the masses.*

 Member of the
Evangelical Christian
Publishers Association

Printed in China.
5 4 3 2 1

Familiar acts are
beautiful through love.

PERCY BYSSHE SHELLEY

Give a little love to a child,
and you get a great deal back.

JOHN RUSKIN

We can't form our children
on our own concepts;
we must take them and love them
as God gives them to us.

JOHANN WOLFGANG VON GOETHE

Choose your love;
love your choice.

THOMAS S. MONSON

Love conquers all things.

VIRGIL

I would rather live and love
where death is king than have
eternal life where love is not.

ROBERT G. INGERSOLL

Love is the circle
that doth restless move
in the same sweet eternity of Love.

ROBERT HERRICK

But as it is written,
Eye hath not seen,
nor ear heard,
neither have entered into the heart of man,
the things which God hath prepared
for them that love him.

1 CORINTHIANS 2:9

Fate, time, occasion, chance, and change?
To these all things are subject but eternal love.

PERCY BYSSHE SHELLEY

To be able to say
how much you love
is to love but little.

PETRARCH

A new commandment I give unto you,
That ye love one another;
as I have loved you,
that ye also love one another.

"Love thy neighbor"
is a precept which could transform the world
if it were universally practiced.

MARY MCLEOD BETHUNE

Brotherly love is
still the distinguishing badge
of every true Christian.

MATTHEW HENRY

Bring love into your home,
for this is where our love
for each other must start.

MOTHER TERESA

There is no exception to
God's commandment
to love everybody.

HENRY BUCKLEW
Daily Spiritual Vitamins

Love must be as much a light
as it is a flame.

HENRY DAVID THOREAU

Love kindled by virtue
always kindles another provided that
its flame appear outwardly.

Love is an act of endless forgiveness,
a tender look which becomes a habit.

PETER USTINOV

People need loving the most when
they deserve it the least.

JOHN HARRIGAN

Freely we serve,
because we freely love,
as in our will to love or not;
in this we stand or fall.

JOHN MILTON

As long as we are loved by others,
I would say we are indispensable;
no man is useless while he has a friend.

ROBERT LOUIS STEVENSON

Nothing we do, however virtuous,
can be accomplished alone;
therefore, we are saved by love.

REINHOLD NIEBUHR

Write down the advice of him
who loves you though you like it not
at the present.

SPANISH PROVERB

No love, no friendship,
can cross the path of our destiny
without leaving some mark on it forever.

He who sows courtesy
reaps friendship, and
he who plants kindness
gathers love.

ST. BASIL

Greater love hath no man than this,
that a man lay down his life for his friends.

JOHN 15:13

The love we give away
is the only love we keep.

ELBERT HUBBARD

Love gives itself;
it is not bought.

HENRY WADSWORTH LONGFELLOW

Love is the greatest thing that God can give us,
for He Himself is love;
and it is the greatest thing we can give to God,
for it will also give ourselves.

JEREMY TAYLOR

All love is sweet,

given or returned.

God gives us love;
something to love He lends us.

ALFRED, LORD TENNYSON

Therefore thou shalt love the LORD thy God,
and keep his charge,
and his statutes, and his judgments,
and his commandments, alway.

DEUTERONOMY 11:1

The measure of God's love is
that He loves without measure.

St. Bernard

God must love the common man;

He made so many of them.

ABRAHAM LINCOLN

The God of love
my Shepherd is.

GEORGE HERBERT

Riches take wings,
comforts vanish, hope withers away,
but love stays with us. God is love.

LEW WALLACE

Jesus said unto him,
Thou shalt love the Lord thy God
with all thy heart,
and with all thy soul,
and with all thy mind.

MATTHEW 22:37

Love is an image of God,
and not a lifeless image,
but the living essence of the divine nature
which beams full of all goodness.

MARTIN LUTHER

The supreme happiness of life is
the conviction that we are loved,
loved for ourselves,
or rather loved in spite of ourselves.

VICTOR HUGO

They say a person needs just three things
to be truly happy in this world:
someone to love,
something to do, and
something to hope for.

TOM BODETT

To love is to
place our happiness in
the happiness of another.

Baron Gottfried Wilhelm von Leibniz

Love one another, and you will be happy.
It's as simple and as difficult as that.

MICHAEL LEUNIG

Love seeks to make happy
rather than to be happy.

RALPH CONNOR

Happiness is the spiritual experience
of living every minute with
love, grace, and gratitude.

DENIS WAITLEY

Joy is love aware of
its own inner happiness.

FULTON J. SHEEN

Love is the master key
which opens the gates of happiness.

OLIVER WENDELL HOLMES

The heart that
has truly loved never forgets.

THOMAS MOORE

And hope maketh not ashamed;
because the love of God is shed abroad
in our hearts by the Holy Ghost
which is given unto us.

ROMANS 5:5

One loving heart
sets another on fire.

St. Augustine

The heart that loves
is always young.

GREEK PROVERB

The heart of him who truly loves
is a paradise on earth;
he has God in himself,
for God is love.

ABBE HUGO FELICITE DE LAMENNAIS

Love is all we have,
the only way that each can help the other.

EURIPIDES

But God commendeth his love toward us,
in that, while we were yet sinners,
Christ died for us.

ROMANS 5:8

Life with Christ is endless love;
without Him it is a loveless end.

Our Savior, who is the Lord above all lords,
would have His servants known by
their badge, which is love.

We love the Lord, of course,
but we often wonder what He finds in us.

EDGAR WATSON HOWE

If we love Christ much,
surely we shall trust Him much.

THOMAS BROOKS

The best portion of a good man's life
is his little, nameless, unremembered
acts of kindness and love.

WILLIAM WORDSWORTH

Life is short.
Be swift to love;
make haste to be kind.

HENRI F. AMIEL

An ounce of love is
worth a pound of knowledge.

We are not made for law,
but for love.

Love is the lesson
which the Lord us taught.

EDMUND SPENCER

Love is the hardest lesson in Christianity,
but for that reason,
it should be the most our care to learn it.

WILLIAM PENN

You will find,
as you look back upon your life,
that the moments when you have really lived
are the moments you have done things
in the spirit of love.

HENRY DRUMMOND

Life is a flower of which
love is the honey.

VICTOR HUGO

We are shaped and fashioned
by what we love.

JOHANN WOLFGANG VON GOETHE

To love and be loved is
to feel the sun
from both sides.

DAVID VISCOTT

To love for the sake of being loved is human,
but to love for the sake of loving is angelic.

Love does not consist of gazing at each other
but in looking together in the same direction.

ANTOINE DE SAINT-EXUPERY

Immature love says,
"I love you because I need you."
Mature love says,
"I need you because I love you."

ERICH FROMM

It is a beautiful necessity
of our nature
to love something.

DOUGLAS JERROLD

I have found the paradox that
if I love until it hurts,
then there is no hurt but only more love.

MOTHER TERESA

One word frees us of all
the weight and pain of life.
That word is love.

SOPHOCLES

Don't hold to anger,
hurt, or pain;
they steal your energy
and keep you from love.

LEO F. BUSCAGLIA

Not father or mother
has loved you as God has,
for it was that you might be happy
He gave His only Son.

HENRY WADSWORTH LONGFELLOW

Love is infallible;
it has no errors,
for all the errors are the want of love.

WILLIAM LAW

It is astonishing
how little one feels poverty
when one loves.

EDWARD BULWER-LYTTON

Who, being loved,
is poor?

Oscar Wilde

Holding the heart of another
in the comforting hands of prayer
is a priceless act of love.

JANET L. WEAVER

The Master,
who loved most of all,
endured the most and
proved His love by His endurance.

HUGH B. BROWN

They do not love that
do not show their love.

WILLIAM SHAKESPEARE

Love is shown in your deeds,
not in your words.

JEROME CUMMINGS

Love looks not with the eyes
but with the mind.

WILLIAM SHAKESPEARE

Blessed is
the influence of one true,
loving soul on another.

GEORGE ELIOT

Joy is the net of love
by which you can catch souls.

MOTHER TERESA

Treasure the love you receive above all.
It will survive long after your gold
and good health have vanished.

OG MANDINO

Between whom there is
hearty truth,
there is love.

Henry David Thoreau

When love and skill work together,

expect a masterpiece.

JOHN RUSKIN

Never forget that the
most powerful force
on earth is love.

NELSON ROCKEFELLER

Love doesn't make the world go around;
love is what makes the ride worthwhile.

FRANKLIN P. JONES

For God so loved the world,
that he gave his only begotten Son,
that whosoever believeth in him
should not perish,
but have everlasting life.

JOHN 3:16

Love is
the river of life
in the world.

HENRY WARD BEECHER